BUILDING YOU!

52 Weekly Devotions of God's Wisdom

Living A Life That Impacts Others!

Levi Rozier

Foreword by Dr. DeLancy A. Dotson

Dedication

This book is dedicated to my wife, Felicia, and to my daughters, Alexis and Harmoni, who support me in everything I do to build others for the Kingdom of God.

Levi Rozier, MTH Senior Pastor
Harvest Builders Worship Center
Warner Robins, Georgia

FOREWORD

When Pastor Levi Rozier asked me to write the foreword for Building You! 52 Weekly Devotions of God's Wisdom, I was honored, elated, and nervous once I realized the great opportunity that I had committed myself to. This book is an important vehicle and task that will be in the hands of millions of God's people. Levi and I crossed paths over twenty years ago as Navy Reservists. We have been connected together ever since. We respect each other like brothers and continue to have great expectations for each other. We are so similar because in everything we do, we operate at an increasingly high level of expectation and with a spirit of excellence.

This book gives me an opportunity to introduce Pastor Levi Rozier and his powerful life-changing wisdom to those who have yet to meet him or hear of him. What better way to experience his anointing, knowledge, wisdom, and spiritual ear than through Building You! 52 Weekly Devotions of God's Wisdom, Living A Life That Impacts Others.

This book is a reflection of Pastor Levi's living, teaching, and beliefs. The weekly reading of this book will serve as a guide for your inspirational study of God's Word. This book will also give you a direct view into Levi the man and his spiritual insight. Prayer, counsel, hope, and encouragement await you within and throughout the pages of this book. Pastor Levi shares wonderful real life lessons and messages that affect our daily lives. As we go through the hustle and bustle of our daily routines, being overwhelmed by the daily challenges of life, what better way to start each week than by seeking God's revelation through His Word.

As God's Spirit is revealed in Pastor Levi's written words, His Power will manifest itself through your victorious living. Allow Pastor Levi's spiritual gifts displayed in this book to penetrate the very depths of your heart, mind, and soul. Yes, this book is about building you. However, this book is also about the affect and impact that YOUR life can and should have on the lives of others.

Dr. DeLancy A. Dotson

CONTENTS

WEEK 1: NO MORE EXCUSES, MAKE THE ADJUSTMENT!

Judges 6:15-16, He said to Him, "O Lord, how shall I deliver Israel? Behold, my family is the least in Manasseh, and I am the youngest in my father's house." 16 But the Lord said to him, "Surely I will be with you, and you shall defeat Midian as one man."

Now is the time says the Lord to stop with the excuses. I did a sermon series a while ago called, "No More Excuses." This same enemy will creep into any person's life during tough times. The excuses from anyone who has not done or will not do what they know God has designed them for will not work. He has given us His grace to make the adjustment so His will can be carried out in our lives. This Word is for fathers, mothers, children, ministers, leaders, coaches, etc.

What if you were not a good father? Well, make the adjustment. Ask for forgiveness. Get into God's Word. Get a mentor. Be a better grandfather. It is time to submit to the will of the Father and godly leadership. Stop with the excuses. What adjustment is God calling for you to make? The kingdom is waiting on you!

* * *

Builder's Prayer

Dear Lord, Please forgive me for living a life less than the one You planned for me. Please forgive me for making excuses. Give me the courage to take the steps necessary for my future in You. I rebuke the spirit of procrastination and excuses from my mind. In Jesus name, I pray. Amen.

WEEK 2: GO TO THE EXPERT!

2 Samuel 5:20, So David came to Baal-perazim and defeated them there; and he said, "The Lord has broken through my enemies before me like the breakthrough of waters." Therefore he named that place Baal-perazim.

Have you ever had a drainage problem in your sink? It starts off small but after a few weeks, it worsens. You try your regular drainage buster but nothing happens. You even try something stronger, still nothing happens. Now you are frustrated and finally decide to call in a plumbing expert. As expected, the drainage problem is solved in a matter of minutes and you get your breakthrough. It may have cost you a little more money to call the expert, but it saved you from further frustration. Have you been waiting for a breakthrough in a certain area in your life?

Friend, it is time to call in the expert for your situation. God is the expert. You must rely upon the written Word of God that is incorruptible. You may be frustrated right now because change has not come, but go to the expert. However, it will cost you. It will cost you time to search the scriptures, patience, and faith; but it will be worth it! This is what David did when he was going out to battle against his enemy. He went to the expert on battle, the Lord Himself. The Lord told him to go up and fight and He would give him the victory. David went up to a place called Baalperazim and the Lord gave him victory there. The word Baalperazim means "breakthrough." The Lord gave David a breakthrough against his enemies. David won because he went to God, the expert. Your breakthrough will come when you trust the expert, God, as well!

* * *

Builder's Prayer

Dear Lord, I ask You for the wisdom to turn to You first before I try to solve my own problems. Thank you that You are the true expert in every area of life where issues may arise. Thank you that my breakthrough is near because I turn to You for the answer. In Jesus name, I pray. Amen.

WEEK 3: JUST DO IT!

Ecclesiastes 9:10, Whatever your hand finds to do, do it with all your might.

One of the major battles a lot of us struggle with is procrastination. We complain when others are not moving fast enough and we make excuses why we are not doing it. We have that someday or one day mentality. We think: One day I am going to stop smoking, get married, apologize to him or her, start my business, go back to school, start saving for my kids college funds, etc. This becomes the song of our lives and nothing ever gets done. A lot of times fear and normalcy set in on us. The routine of life traps us in.

We must take the step of faith and obey God. No more excuses. I know Nike thought they were the original ones to come up with the phrase "Just Do It." But the Word of God has been speaking this to all of us. We should just do it and do it with all our heart. However, I am not just talking about what we are striving to become. We should also be faithful and work hard on what we are responsible for right now. Don't be foolish in your steps by disregarding your priorities. Just take the step of action towards your goals. Examine where you are in your life right now regarding your goals. Ask God about what He wants you to do or keep doing. Then, just do it.

* * *

Builder's Prayer

Dear Lord, Please help me to defeat the spirit of procrastination in my life. Help me to be bold and energized in my pursuit towards the goals in life you've given me. Help me to be proactive in managing the responsibilities that you've trusted in my hands. In Jesus name, I pray. Amen.

WEEK 4: DON'T LET THE ENEMY PULL THE POWER CORD!

Proverbs 3:5, Trust in the LORD with all your heart and do not lean on your own understanding.

Have you ever worked on a laptop and the power bar became very low indicating you need to use the power cord? Then you plug the cord into the socket to get power. As you start to type again, you move and without knowing it, you are unplugged again. You don't realize that the power cord is no longer connected to the outlet until the laptop shuts down. The move you made unplugged you from the power source. The enemy does not want you to live your day powered by God. With all of his might, he will try to pull us from God's power socket with the circumstances and cares of this world. Stay plugged into God by reading His Word daily, connecting with godly people, and declaring God's Word over your life. Regardless of the presence of clouds/circumstances in your life, the sun/Son powers you and gives you light.

* * *

Builder's Prayer

Dear Lord, Forgive me for letting the circumstances in my life keep me from spending time with You. Help me to stay focused on You and Your wonderful love for me. Help me to see that You are the only true power in my life. Without You, I can do nothing. In Jesus name, I pray. Amen.

WEEK 5: EMBRACE THE BANNER!

Song of Solomon 2:4, ...and His banner over me is love.

Have you ever been in a situation where you thought that you might not measure up to the environment the Lord placed you in? When God places you in a certain position, you know it was His grace and love that got you there. Yes, you may be talented, but you know that if it had not been for God's intervention, it would not have happened. When you arrive in that place, you might not have what others have right now. All you may have is the bare minimum, the Father's love and His Word.

This is all the lady had who was in love with King Solomon in Song of Solomon. She gave the metaphor of going to a banquet where the other ladies there were a little more prestigious than she was. They had canopies over their heads that kept the sun off of them and someone was caring for them. However, she was not envious or worried about what others had or who thought that she did not belong because the banner of Solomon's love was over her head. She also embraced the love and the pressure of what she did not have because his love had her covered. This is an encouraging word for us today. Jeremiah 31:3 says that God has loved us with an everlasting love. Embrace the banner of love the Father has placed over you. When things are not going as well as they should and life is telling you that you don't belong, embrace His love and walk in confidence. Embrace His love and also share His love with others.

* * *

Builder's Prayer

Dear Lord, Please help me to see that Your love is sufficient for me in all circumstances. When I feel inadequate, please remind me that Your love for me makes me adequate for all good things that You give me. Please strengthen my confidence in You. In Jesus name, I pray. Amen.

WEEK 6: LET THE PEACE OF GOD RULE!

Colossians 3:15, Let the peace of Christ rule in your hearts.....

I know we live in a busy world and a lot is happening to us and around us. I had a friend who was having some problems in their relationship. As the person began to talk to me, I became concerned because they were having problems sleeping at night. They felt they had done everything God had required them to do in the relationship but there was no peace. At night, they would have dreams of people making fun of them and there was wrestling. Even though my friend was going to bed on time and thought they were fine, their soul man was not fine. Our "soul man" consists of our mind, will, and emotions and can become unsettled. This is where the devil will deal with a lot of us. The enemy deals with us all at this level because he does not want us living in peace.

I advised this person to do what David did and as he instructed us to do in Psalms 34:2 when he said, "My soul will boast in the Lord." David was commanding his soul to do something, which was to bless the Lord even though he did not feel like it. We can also command our soul to rest at night in Jesus name. We have to tell our mind and emotions to be at peace in Jesus name and allow the angels of God to do their work. Don't allow the enemy or anyone else to steal your peace. Command your soul to be still. Declare peace to your mind and let it rule your heart. Let God's Word come alive in you. For the next thirty days, try reading Colossians 3 before you go to bed. I declare God's favor and blessing over your life!

* * *

Builder's Prayer

Dear Lord, I declare that my mind, will, and emotions are in perfect peace according to the Word of God. Thank you for keeping me in the Peace that only You can give. You are Peace and I declare Your Peace in my soul. I am more than a conqueror in You! In Jesus name, I pray. Amen.

WEEK 7: DON'T HOLD BACK!

Isaiah 54:2, Enlarge the place of your tent; stretch out the curtains of your dwellings, spare not.

Our humanity causes us to hold back when people have abused our love and trust. This normally involves relationships where trust was established but then hurt or disappointment occurred. All of us may have experienced this. It is true that trust must be earned and that feelings must be protected. What we don't want to do is to get bitter and hold back the love we are supposed to display towards each other. The Bible gives us instruction about loving people. God does not want us to hold back. Matthew 5:46 says, "For if you love those who love you, what reward will you have?"

God wants us to love those who have hurt us. We are not flattering God when we only love those who love us. He has never held back His love from us, even when we were unlovable. It takes faith to love those who have hurt you because some people have cut your soul man deeply. However, for your own sake, you must push forward and love like God loves. Don't hold back your love because there is a dying world that needs it.

* * *

Builder's Prayer

Dear Lord, Please help me to love others unconditionally. Help me to love others past my own pain and disappointment. Please give me the grace to forgive those who have hurt me as You forgive me for any pain I have caused others. Give me the strength to love. In Jesus name, I pray. Amen.

WEEK 8: PAYING ATTENTION!

Philippians 2:4, Do not merely look out for your own personal interests, but also for the interests of others.

We live in a society where we don't pay close attention to the needs of others unless we are forced to. In some cases, we take the "see" and "don't see" approach. Not too long ago, much attention was given to Haiti because of the earthquake that damaged the country. The tragedy forced countries and nations around the world to focus their attention on the needs of the people. This was good, but unfortunately the need for resources and governmental intervention has existed in Haiti for years. The earthquake just forced everyone to pay attention.

We must do a better job at paying attention to the needs of people around us. People are hurting and are facing challenges that they have never faced before. People are displaying their hurt through different avenues. God cares deeply about us. He is truly paying attention to our needs. He desires that we display and care about the needs of each other. One of the major needs of all of us is the need to be loved. Please don't hold back your love or retaliate against others who have hurt you. Pay attention and display the love of God to the people around you. Do it now and let God be glorified!

* * *

Builder's Prayer

Dear Lord, Give me eyes like Yours so that I can see the needs of others. Help me to be mindful of the lives of those around me so I can be a blessing in their lives and not an obstacle. Thank you for giving me a discerning spirit for people in need. Help me to love. In Jesus name, I pray. Amen.

WEEK 9: A LOAN TO THE LORD!

Proverbs 19:17, One who is gracious to a poor man lends to the Lord, and He will repay him for his good deed.

The Lord is seriously concerned about how we treat one another. Times are hard for people. People are being challenged emotionally, financially, physically, and in so many other areas. God is truly concerned about the intricate details of our lives. People need the touch of God and you are the one to touch them. The woman with a bleeding problem touched Jesus and was healed. Jesus now wants to touch people through us.

Proverbs 19 speaks of what God does for those who are in need and how He rewards those who help meet those needs. When we show kindness to each other, we are giving to the Lord. He will not be in debt to any person. Begin to look for people to show kindness to. When you do kind things for others, God sees it. Your kindness to others does not go unnoticed. God cares for you and will bless you as you look for ways to build people.

* * *

Builder's Prayer

Dear Lord, Help me to be kind to others. Help me to discern the needs and pain that others are dealing with. Please give me the grace to love in a way that reflects who You are in me. When people look at me, please let them see You in me. In Jesus name, I pray. Amen.

WEEK 10: HE WILL QUIET YOU!

Zephaniah 3:17, The Lord your God is in your midst, a victorious warrior.
He will exult over you with joy, He will be quiet in His love,
He will rejoice over you with shouts of joy.

L ife is full of uncertainties and cares that affect people in different ways. The devil's desire is to make a lot of noise in our soul man (mind, will, and emotions) so that we will doubt God and not embrace His love. This can be done through the hurts, pains, and challenges we face. God is concerned about us and understands the noise that is trying to drown out His love towards us. Because we live in a sinful world, we will have challenges. The Lord wants us to know what the Prophet Zephaniah was speaking to God's people. Our God is with us and He wants to quiet us with His love.

If you embrace the Father's love and understand that He loves you, it will give you peace and quiet your soul man. Your mind will begin to rest in His love. Whatever challenges you may face, you will know that God is with you and that you can trust His love. However, you must also let the love flow out of you to help bring rest to others. God is awesome! God is mighty and will save us!

* * *

Builder's Prayer

Dear Lord, Thank you for the quiet in my soul that only you can give. Help me to be a light for others to see the peace that only you can give. Thank you for helping me to love others. Thank you for peace in my mind, will, and emotions. Thank you for Your love. In Jesus name, I pray. Amen.

WEEK 11: DON'T GET BOXED IN!

---

*Colossians 2:3, In whom are hidden all the treasures of
wisdom and knowledge.*

Many local organizations use state and federal money to help support programs. Sometimes the money is not there. I was a part of an organization for children that experienced the same lack of resources. During a meeting, the members of the organization were despondent over the lack of resources because they had a passion for helping children. While sitting in the meeting, the Lord spoke strongly to me and I conveyed what I heard to the team. I stated, "The money may be drying up, but our innovative ideas have not." I continued to tell them that this was not the time to give in, but to raise the bar for helping children. We needed to come out of our comfort zone and allow God to stretch the team. This was the time to tap into new resources, create new relationships, increase our area of influence, look at who was at the table, etc. We had been boxed in for a while. We became comfortable with thinking that the money would be there every year.

Builder, I don't know where you are financially or where you may be in your career, but whatever God has placed in your heart to do, do it. Do not let money be an issue. God is looking for someone who will dare to believe and trust Him. The things we have put our trust in are drying up, but God is eternal and so are His ideas and concepts. Do not allow the devil to get you boxed in like a chicken or bird in a cage. You are an eagle and it is time to soar in your thoughts and actions. Let the wisdom of God come alive in your heart! The scriptures say, all the treasure of wisdom and knowledge are in Christ. If you are His child, you have unlimited resources! God is with us and if you don't know Him, ask Him into your heart afresh and receive His wisdom.

* * *

Builder's Prayer

Dear Lord, Give me the courage to step out and up into bigger dreams and to do what You created me to do. When challenges come my way, give me the wisdom I need to find another way, a better way, towards Your goals for my life. In Jesus name, I pray. Amen.

WEEK 12: MAKE THE EXCHANGE!

---

2 Corinthians 5:21, He made Him who knew no sin to be sin on our behalf, so that we might become the righteousness of God in Him.

Have you ever had something happen to you or you did something wrong where you deserved the punishment that came with it? It's like driving over glass in the road knowing there is glass in the road and your tire goes flat. There is no one to blame for the situation but yourself. Then all of a sudden, someone comes along and tells you that they have a new tire for you that is paid for. All you will have to do is make an exchange. None of us would turn down this offer! It may be hard to believe that a person would exchange a new tire for an old damaged tire.

This is what Christ has done for each of us. He did not know any sin, but we were sinful. So He took onto Himself our old dirty habits and in exchange, He gave us a new life. This allowed us to become righteous. Still, the devil does all he can to confuse us. He doesn't want us to think that we are righteous, because of the things we have done. The death, burial, and resurrection of Jesus are too powerful. We must make the exchange now! Exchange our sin for His righteousness, our sickness for His healing, our hurts and emotional scars for His peace. We must receive it by faith and be willing to give up our old life to make the exchange.

* * *

Builder's Prayer

Dear Lord, Help me to see the exchange that Jesus made so that I may be made righteous in Your sight. Thank you for the death, burial, and resurrection of Jesus that gives me eternal life. Thank you for Your love that is stronger than my sin. In Jesus name, I pray. Amen.

WEEK 13: THE SIDE EFFECTS OF TAKING GOD'S MEDICINE!

Proverbs 4:20 and 22, My son, give attention to my words; incline your ear to my sayings...For they are life to those who find them and health to all their body.

Most of the time, when doctors give you medication, they warn you of the different side effects. Also, when you have to take prescribed medicine, doctors tell you how often to take it to get the maximum desired results. When we disobey the doctor's directive, we may not get the results or benefits from the medication. Medicine was designed to diagnose, prevent, and aid healing. The Lord's Word, the Bible, is a medicine that needs to be taken daily. Proverbs 4:20 and 22, tells us, "My son, give attention to my words; incline your ear to my sayings...For they are life to those who find them and health to all their body." When this medicine is taken daily, you are sure to have some serious side effects. The implication of this is...if you don't take God's medicine, you will also have serious side effects.

Life is tough and things are happening all around you. You need God's Word daily. Just as you would not take a whole bottle of pills at once, you must also take your time to take in and absorb God's Word. If you are dealing with a situation, take God's Word and meditate on it. If you are concerned about your destiny, go to the Word of God; take it in and begin to speak what the Word of God is saying about you. You are God's champion in the earth and God wants you well in every area of your life. He cares for you and has given you free access to His Word. You don't have to worry about the high cost of God's medication because it was paid for with the blood of Jesus.

* * *

Builder's Prayer

Dear Lord, Thank you for Your written Word that is medicine for my spirit, healing for my body, and wholeness for my mind. Help me to see that I have time each day to give to You regardless of the circumstances in my life. Thank you for giving me instructions for life. In Jesus name, I pray. Amen.

WEEK 14: GOD WANTS US TO TOUCH PEOPLE!

Luke 8:43-44, And a woman who had a hemorrhage for twelve years, and could not be healed by anyone, came up behind Him and touched the fringe of His cloak, and immediately her hemorrhage stopped.

Touching Jesus allows people to touch you. There was a woman in the Bible who had spent all she had trying to be healed of a bleeding condition. She heard about Jesus and wanted to touch Him as He passed by. Though the crowd was heavy, she pressed her way through and connected with Jesus by touching His garment. This woman was instantly made well because of her faith and tenacity. When we make Jesus the Lord of our life, people should be connecting with us and lives should be changing; as we walk through the work place or as we have conversations with people. Not because we are God, but because He is living in us and has placed us here to affect change in the earth by building people.

Don't think you are not worthy enough to impact people's lives because you are. You must see yourself through the eyes of Jesus: whole, awesome, a new person, and a person walking in love and victory! This week you must know that you can affect change in the earth because you are connected to Jesus, and people can connect with you. You cannot say that the Lord has not blessed you recently with the need to share or to touch the heart of others. God blessed you to be a blessing. Touch people with your love, kind words, friendship, by listening, or with a gift. As you touch people, this allows God to touch their hearts. Be strong and build people!

* * *

Builder's Prayer

Dear Lord, I want to be a blessing to others. Thank you for blessing me. Show me how to share Your love with others. My greatest desire is to touch You so that I can bless others. Let Your light shine in my heart as I go out and build people wherever I meet them. In Jesus name, I pray. Amen.

WEEK 15: FILE BANKRUPTCY!

Matthew 5:3, Blessed are the poor in spirit,
for theirs is the kingdom of heaven.

When we hear the term "bankrupt" or that someone has "filed bankruptcy," it is always used with a negative connotation. Bankruptcy is defined as the legally declared inability of an individual or organization to pay its creditors. This means that the person needs serious help or guidance with their current financial situation. The Bible indirectly speaks about us filing bankruptcy in a positive way. The scripture says in Matthew 5:3 that you're blessed when you're at the end of your rope or you are blessed when you declare spiritual bankruptcy. The King James Bible says, "Blessed are the poor in Spirit." Jesus is telling us that He cannot truly intervene in our lives unless we declare bankruptcy. Remember, bankruptcy is the inability to make something happen. Jesus wants us to rely on His power to make things happen. Our ability is limited. We must file bankruptcy. Jesus wants us to empty ourselves so that He can rule in our spirit and in our situation.

You may be at the end of your rope in a situation and cannot fix it on your own. 1 Peter 5:7 states, "God cares for you, so turn all your worries over to him." What you need to do is file bankruptcy. You are trying to control everything and everybody. You need to let God rule in your emotions and situations. Before God can rule, He needs you to first file bankruptcy. God cares for you. Release control and allow Him to rule.

* * *

Builder's Prayer

Dear Lord, Help me to let go and let You rule in my life. I cannot do anything apart from You. Please help me to see that I can do and be so much more in Your strength. Thank you that You are already working all things out for my good and Your glory. In Jesus name, I pray. Amen.

WEEK 16: CARE CASTER!

---

1 Peter 5:7, Casting all your anxiety on Him because He cares for you.

I t is time to get aggressive. Everyone faces different challenges and sometimes the cares of this world seem to weigh us down. Some of the challenges people face are new and some are familiar. It becomes very dangerous when we become too familiar with our circumstances or challenges. One of Jesus's strongest followers, Peter, was familiar with Jesus. However, when Jesus gave His disciples a directive that challenged their thinking, they proved that they were more familiar with their challenges than Jesus Himself. They had been fishing all day and caught no fish. Jesus told them to go out and try it again. This challenged Peter's thinking because he was a fisherman by trade and was familiar with the challenges of fishing. Jesus wanted him to cast those cares on Him and follow His directive. We must become what my wife Felicia calls a "Care Caster."

God wants us to take our situations and push them off us and throw them on Him. When the cares of life are trying to weigh you down mentally, emotionally, or physically, you must become a Care Caster. When you cast your cares on Him, you need to receive what He has for you in its place. When you cast your fears of sickness on

Him, receive your healing from Him; when you cast your cares of doubt and unbelief on Him, receive your faith. Builder, God does not want to just take your cares from you. He also wants to give you peace and success in return. I am praying and believing that you are a Care Caster. Begin throwing those cares today!

* * *

Builder's Prayer

Dear Lord, Help me to become a Care Caster so that I can give my concerns and cares to You. You are my refuge and my strength. I believe that You are able to lift my worries and ease my burdens...mentally, emotionally and physically. Almighty God, I trust You. In Jesus name, I pray. Amen.

WEEK 17: EXPOSE OUR FEARS!

John 1:4-5, In Him was life, and the life was the Light of men. The Light shines in the darkness, and the darkness did not comprehend it.

We all like taking pictures and showing them to friends and family. The older cameras required us to take film to the store so it could be developed. The process of developing pictures involves putting the film in a dark room and working through the process to get them to develop. There is a certain period of time that it must remain in the dark room for the pictures to be perfect. Light is an enemy to the process of developing pictures. Exposing film to the light will destroy the picture. This metaphor explains what we must do with our fears. We must take our fears out of the dark rooms of our heart; where they are being developed and expose them to the light. When we keep our fears a secret or don't confront challenges, the images and the force behind it become stronger and clearer. It causes us to make excuses for why we will not move forward in life and it holds us back from even trying. When we allow these fears to develop, they become a picture in our spirit and soul.

We must bring our fears out of the dark room and expose them to the light of God's Word so they can be destroyed. There are some fears that have been in your darkroom (secret place) for a long time: the fear of failure, fear of rejection, fear of the worst case scenario, fear of being alone, fear of not being loved, fear of not mattering or fear of someone finding out that you are afraid. I want to encourage you to bring that fear to the light by admitting that it exists and to bring it out before God with honesty. Look up the scriptures in God's Word that speak to your fears and act in faith. You may be shaking in your boots, but you must do something. Don't allow fear to stop you another day!

* * *

Builder's Prayer
Dear Lord, Shine Your light in my heart to expose the fears in my life. Help me to overcome the fear and anxiety that is keeping me from moving forward in my life. I trust You to help me live with a spirit of courage. In Jesus name, I pray. Amen.

WEEK 18: GOD'S APPROVAL!

Hebrews 11:6, And without faith it is impossible to please Him, for he who comes to God must believe that He is and that He is a rewarder of those who seek Him.

P eople are always looking for man's approval. We change the way we dress, talk, act, and sometimes, we forget who we are. Seeking man's approval all the time can be unhealthy. You should seek God's approval. The scripture says, to get God's approval, all you have to do is have faith in Him. And when you look for His approval and seek after Him, He will reward you. There is nothing wrong with wanting to be accepted and loved when it is connected to God. You are an awesome person and the only approval you need is God's approval and everything else will line up. This is truly the time to put your trust in God. If you seek God's approval, you will be rewarded and not put to shame. Keep the faith today and do not be discouraged, because you are a winner!

* * *

Builder's Prayer

Dear Lord, You have already approved me. I will use the power You placed on the inside of me to walk boldly in life. I embrace the fact that You love me unconditionally and that You will reward me for seeking You. Give me the courage to be who You created me to be. In Jesus name, I pray. Amen.

WEEK 19: IT'S TIME TO BE RELIGIOUS!

James 1:27, Pure and undefiled religion in the sight of our God and Father is this: to visit orphans and widows in their distress, and to keep oneself unstained by the world.

In our culture, we define religion sometimes in a way that God never intended. We make statements like, "There he or she goes being religious again." We make these statements based on what a person says or does or by what denominational group they are a part of. When we do this, we give the word "religious" a negative connotation. People begin to frown on the word, and do not want to be called religious. Recently, I took a trip to Haiti and visited a lot of orphans and widows to meet their needs. When you search the scriptures for the meaning of religion, James gives a clear definition of what it is. James says it is to visit the fatherless (orphans) and the widows in their affliction.

This is what religion is and not what we have created it to be in our religious culture. God is concerned about the orphans and widows around us. When you get involved with a child's life, you are considered religious and this we should not frown on or shun away from. God is concerned about those who cannot defend themselves. I want to encourage you to become religious today. Don't miss the opportunity to allow God to work through you in the area where you live, worship, or work. You don't have to go far to be religious. Embark on a religious trip to visit an orphan or a widow for God.

* * *

Builder's Prayer

Dear Lord, Give me a heart that is like Your heart. Help me to do Your work for those who cannot do for themselves. Give me a Word to share and the love to give to orphans and widows as I seek opportunities to touch the lives of others. In Jesus name, I pray. Amen.

WEEK 20: ADVANCEMENT!

---

1 Corinthians 3:6, I planted, Apollos watered, but God was causing the growth.

Have you been praying for a love one's life to change and it seems like there is no advancement? Or are you involved in a relationship where it seems like the more you pray or do for that person, things are just not changing? Today, I want to encourage you to keep doing what you are doing. Never think that what you are doing in love and kindness is in vain, especially when you want a person's heart to turn towards God. And yes, there will be times of frustration and disappointment, but you have to know that things are advancing. Paul gave a great example in scripture about people's lives being changed. The people were arguing about who was better, Paul or Apollos. Paul broke it down this way to encourage your heart: "I planted, Apollos watered, but God was causing the growth." When you do your part, God will do His part. As you love people and treat people right, you are planting a seed for change. God will send someone else to water the seed you planted and before you know it, there is life change! It does not matter who gets the credit, just know that as you do your part, things are advancing in that person's life for God to ultimately change them.

God cares about people and He wants to use you to advance His kingdom. Will you do your part today?

* * *

Builder's Prayer
Dear Lord, Equip me to do my part to advance Your Kingdom. Give me Your eyes to see the needs of the people. Give me Your heart to love everyone. Give me Your strength to carry the message to as many people as I can for as long as my life will allow. In Jesus name, I pray. Amen.

WEEK 21: DO NOT GET COMFORTABLE!

Isaiah 41:10, Do not fear, for I am with you; do not anxiously look about you, for I am your God. I will strengthen you, surely I will help you, surely I will uphold you with My righteous right hand.

E veryone has been impacted by the changing economy, which makes us reassess our financial situations. This is not a bad thing to do in itself, because we should know where we are financially. But the economy and circumstances around us have stopped us from dreaming or thinking big. No one wants to lose or take setbacks, but fear has a lot of us settling for what is and not moving in the direction God has called us to. To quote Fredrick Wilcox, "Progress involves risk, and you cannot steal second base and keep your feet on first." A lot of us have made it to first base in our ministry, finances, marriage, business, education, etc. but we know God is requiring more out of us. Sometimes we look at the situation and we say we are waiting for the right time, or for things to get better. However, God is saying to us, "Do not get comfortable with where you are."

We obeyed and trusted God before and it got us to first base, but we have stayed on first base too long and got comfortable. We are afraid that things might not work out for us because everything is telling us that we should stay where we are. Just like the baseball player who listens to his first base coach on when to go to the next base, you should listen to your coach, God and His Word, and step out. Dream again! Step out into what God has called you to do! You will succeed! The God in you will get you through; just do not get comfortable with where you are.

* * *

Builder's Prayer

Dear Lord, Renew my passion for life. Help me to see new ways to do things and new things to do. Every day is a blessing! Help me to not take each day lightly but to give thanks to You. I will worship You with my life and not get comfortable with where I am. In Jesus name, I pray. Amen.

WEEK 22: HEAR THE MESSAGE!

Romans 10:16-17, However, they did not all heed the good news; for Isaiah says, "Lord, who has believed our report?" So faith comes from hearing, and hearing by the word of Christ.

There are so many different ways messages are being conveyed to us. We receive them by radio, email, television, texts, books, conversation, etc. All of these are great ways to receive and hear a message. As we hear a message, we must be careful to discern what the message is conveying to us. The Word of God is telling you or sending you a message that you are healed, blessed, wise, and mighty. But the messages from your past, your enemy, and even your television may be sending you a wrong message. Be encouraged to hear and receive the message from God's Word. If the other messages you are hearing are contrary to what the Word says about you, it is time to hear the message from God's Word more. The more you hear the message, the more you will believe it. God loves you and you are a champion! It's one thing for others to say it about you, but you really hear it when you say it.

* * *

Builder's Prayer

Dear Lord, Help me to hear Your Word in my heart. I believe what Your Word says about me. I am the righteousness of God and I am healed in my mind, body, and spirit. Give me the strength to live as a champion and not defeated. You are my God and I am a champion in You! In Jesus name, I pray. Amen.

WEEK 23: RECOGNIZE!

Isaiah 61:9,...All who see them will recognize them because they are the offspring whom the Lord has blessed.

The scripture above is referring to God making a change in your life where others will recognize the transformation. You could be dealing with some things that held you back (fear, worry, anxiety, etc.) and affected you in so many areas. You may have been second guessing yourself or you may be in a place financially or emotionally that has been weighing you down. God's children were in that place and He came and declared a blessing over them. He wanted to reassure them that He had not forgotten about them. God even told them, "I will give you double (blessing) for your trouble and shame." And all who see them will recognize the blessing on you. This is what happens when you keep yourself connected to His Word and what He is doing in your life. No, we are not perfect and they were not. However, during their time of distress, they trusted God. Trust God and His Word. Whatever you are facing or encountering right now, people will and are going to recognize that you are one the Lord has blessed. They know your situation and there will be no other way to explain the blessing on your life. Continue to stay connected to His Word and your purpose. People will recognize!

* * *

Builder's Prayer

Dear Lord, Help me to stay connected to Your Word and the purpose You had in mind when You created me. I believe that You will bless my life in a way that others will recognize that You are my God. Thank you for accepting me and my imperfections. In Jesus name, I pray. Amen.

WEEK 24: HE KNOWS WHAT HE IS DOING!

John 13:7, Jesus answered and said to him, "What I do you do not realize now, but you will understand hereafter."

We have all faced situations or are facing situations, and we want to ask God "why?" We cannot seem to get our minds around why God allows certain things to happen in our lives. I wish I had an answer for you, but I would be over stepping my boundaries. When Jesus was about to go to the cross, His disciples and friends did not understand what was about to happen to Him and could not get their minds around it either. But they did understand God's plan later. Sometimes you do not understand what God is allowing or doing in your life. There are some things God will allow you to understand during your time here on earth. But there will be some things you will not understand until you see Him face to face. You must trust God because He loves you and knows what He is doing. Give your life and everything you are involved in totally to Him and let Him run the show.

* * *

Builder's Prayer

Dear Lord, Thank you for being a strategic God. I may not understand everything going on in my life but You are God over my circumstances. Give me the strength and patience to trust You even when I can't trace you. You are amazing God! In Jesus name, I pray. Amen.

WEEK 25: DO IT ANYWAY!

---

2 Timothy 1:7 For God has not given us a spirit of timidity, but of power and love and discipline.

F ear is a tool that the enemy uses to hold us back or paralyze us from achieving God's best for us. Unfortunately, it works sometimes. Fear stops us from accomplishing some of the God-given desires that we know in our hearts God has called us to do. After going so long without stepping out, we become complacent and settle for the status quo. We have success breathing in us and we need to do it anyway in spite of fear. I remember when I asked for my wife's hand in marriage, I was so afraid. In my heart, I knew God had placed her in my heart but the only thing that separated me from being with her was me asking her father. I don't know if I was afraid of him or if I feared rejection. Whichever it was, all I know is that fear had grabbed me but I decided to do it anyway. You have to do it anyway; even if you are shaking in your boots. Sometimes you think that fear has to leave you completely before you act. No, sometimes you have to do it afraid in order for fear to leave. You must recognize it; admit you are afraid and then do it anyway. God is with you and He will never leave or forsake you. So, whatever it is God is calling you to do, do it anyway.

* * *

Builder's Prayer

Dear Lord, Please give me the courage to do all that You are calling me to do. Even if I am afraid, I want to do it anyway. Help me to remain focused on Your power. Thank you for empowering me with the grace to do it anyway. I can do all things with Your help. In Jesus name, I pray. Amen.

WEEK 26: BELIEVE AGAIN FOR HE IS ABLE!

Ephesians 3:20, Now to Him who is able to do far more abundantly beyond all that we ask or think, according to the power that works within us.

L ife can be tough sometimes. When we have set backs, we stop dreaming and believing for God's greatest. We even give up on what we know that God has told us to do. The tough times we are facing as a nation and as a people can present an opportunity for God to do something great in our lives if we just believe and dream again. Builder, we must know that God is able! You have to push pass the setbacks and failures because the situation may have changed but the God we serve remains the same. The scripture today is a powerful message to inspire you to dream and believe again. It is time to stop sitting in the shadow of the success of others and start believing and allowing God to do more than you can ask or think about. Do not allow disappointments, depression, oppression, or delays make you doubt God's plan for you and your family. There is more in store for you if you can believe it. Be excited about your future and what God has planned for you! His Word shall be fulfilled in your life!

* * *

Builder's Prayer

Dear Lord, Renew Your hope in my heart. Help me to believe again in Your plan and purpose for my life. You are a great God with a great plan. You are a God of restoration. Restore my dreams and my expectations for a great life in You. In Jesus name, I pray. Amen.

WEEK 27: GOING THE EXTRA MILE!

---

1 Timothy 3:1, It is a trustworthy statement: if any man aspires to the office of overseer, it is a fine work he desires to do.

The office of a Bishop is an honorable position that brings great responsibility. This person must strive to walk in integrity and shun the appearance of anything that would give others the impression that he is not. This is called going the extra mile. I know you are not a Bishop, but you are an Overseer / Bishop over whatever ministry, business, family, or team God graced you to be in charge of. You are not perfect, but you must try to go the extra mile for the sake of those who are watching you. I want to encourage you to remain true to yourself and to God. Go the extra mile for the benefit of those who don't believe or who may be mismanaging their faith. I know it may cause you to go out of your way, but people need to see Jesus in you.

* * *

Builder's Prayer

Dear Lord, Please give me the wisdom and the strength to give more than what is expected in all areas of my life. You are able to grace me with the ability to give more. I believe that with Your grace, I can go the extra mile so that You can receive the glory for Your presence in my life. In Jesus name, I pray. Amen.

WEEK 28: LIFETIME WARRANTY!

Psalm 30:5, For His anger is but for a moment, His favor is for a lifetime. Weeping may last for the night, but a shout of joy comes in the morning.

When we purchase a new item it normally comes with a one or two-year warranty. It is temporary and it won't last for a lifetime. This is the opposite with God's favor. When we go through life and experience pain and disappointment, it is only temporary. But the favor of God is for a lifetime! Because of Jesus Christ, God's favor does not have to be renewed. You have been favored and it won't run out!

* * *

Builder's Prayer
Dear Lord, Thank you for Your favor in my life. Your favor is eternal and is an assurance to me that negative circumstances are temporary. Thank you that Your favor in my life is new every day. In Jesus name, I pray. Amen.

WEEK 29: BELIEVE GOD'S WORD!

Romans 3:4, May it never be! Rather, let God be found true, though every man be found a liar.

We must believe God's Word to be true regardless of whether man believes it or if the circumstance or situation is contrary to what the Word says. Whether that sickness or situation is getting better or not, let God's Word be true. God's Word says you are healed, you have peace, you have greatness inside of you, and you are blessed. Whose report will you believe? Choose to believe the Father today and be encouraged. Life is tough sometimes. It is not easy because the pain seems closer than God. Have faith and trust God. Believe the truth!

* * *

Builder's Prayer
Dear Lord, Help me to believe Your Word. Help me to navigate around my doubts back to the truth of Your Word. You are my resource of truth. Thank you for patiently waiting on me to see You in all of Your truth. In Jesus name, I pray. Amen.

WEEK 30: GET A CLEAR PICTURE!

Matthew 17:17, And Jesus answered and said, "You unbelieving and perverted generation..."

When we drive our vehicles and notice that our windshield has numerous bugs on it from traveling, we immediately clean it off. We understand that if we do not get it cleaned, it will distort our view of what is ahead. This is what the enemy tries to do to us through life's circumstances. The devil's desire is to distort our thinking about who God is and what He can do through us. We must admit that we have all been victims of the enemy's plot one time or another through our hurts and disappointments. We must continually make frequent stops in God's Word to cleanse the windshield of our soul. This will help rid us of the perverse thinking about God, people, church, etc. It is time to be healed in our thinking by casting down every vain imagination. You are victorious!

* * *

Builder's Prayer

Dear Lord, Please elevate my mind as I read Your Word. Help me to see You clearly so that I can see myself and others clearly as well. Help me to respond appropriately in all situations with a clear perspective and in love. In Jesus name, I pray. Amen.

WEEK 31: CHOOSE NOT TO SUBMIT!

Galatians 5:1, It was for freedom that Christ set us free; therefore keep standing firm and do not be subject again to a yoke of slavery.

We are always being encouraged to submit to those who have rule over us or submit to the Word of God. Here, the Word is telling us NOT to submit. Our past hurts, failures, habits, hang ups, or traditions want to keep us in bondage even though we are free. Rise up and stop submitting to the things that are holding you back. You are not perfect, but tell those things to submit to you through the Word of God in Jesus Name. You are free and healed NOW!

* * *

Builder's Prayer
Dear Lord, Please guide me away from submitting to those things that are holding me back from a full life in You. Grant me the strength to boldly declare that I am free in You. Thank you for Your power in my life as I submit myself to Your Word. In Jesus name, I pray. Amen.

WEEK 32: LOVE IS IN THE AIR!

John 3:16, For God so loved the world, that He gave His only begotten Son, that whoever believes in Him shall not perish, but have eternal life.

Love is so amazing! It always brings out the best in people. The initiator of love did that to us when He sent His son to die for us. This love has been in the air since mankind was created and God wants this love to penetrate our hearts. When His love penetrates our hearts, it begins to work through us. Love is in the air, but the originator of love wants to get it out of the air and into our hearts. Loving people is what our God does best. He wants us to show love to others. Loving God and Loving People. Love strong today!

* * *

Builder's Prayer
Dear Lord, Thank you God for Your love for me. Help me to love like You and to show Your love to others in a great way. I want to bring glory to You by being an example of Your love in the earth. Help me to love others in a way that is pleasing to You. In Jesus name, I pray. Amen.

WEEK 33: OBEY THE SOUND!

---

1 Kings 18:41, Now Elijah said to Ahab, "Go up, eat and drink; for there is the sound of the roar of a heavy shower."

There is a sound that God is speaking on the inside of you (in your spirit) and you need to make the necessary adjustments. That sound is the voice of the Lord for: vision, your gift, your marriage, business, ministry, purpose, and direction. There has been some dry area in your life and God is telling you to prepare yourself for the rain of breakthrough. When you obey the sound, God will empower you to do things that are beyond your capability. Get ready and obey the sound!

* * *

Builder's Prayer
Dear Lord, Help me to obey Your sound for my life. I believe that there is a sound of abundance flowing through my life from You. I am ready to obey Your instructions for my life today. In Jesus name, I pray. Amen.

WEEK 34: DO NOT SILENCE THE WORD!

Mark 7:13, Thus invalidating the word of God by your tradition which you have handed down; and you do many things such as that.

We must be on guard against the perfunctory and traditions of life, good or bad. If our traditions or stubborn habits are keeping the Word of God from being active in our lives, we must change. God's Word is quick and powerful, but we can silence it. When the Word of God has the freedom to be loud in our lives, it will challenge the norm and silence the traditions of life. You need to examine your life and see where the Word is silent because of your traditions. Let the Word of God make some noise! You are healed! You are prosperous! Your mind is alert! You have favor with God and Man!!

* * *

Builder's Prayer
Dear Lord, Please give me the wisdom to recognize the traditions and routines that threaten to override my relationship with You. Please keep me

focused on the power and life in Your Word. I want to keep my relationship with You the priority in my life. In Jesus name, I pray. Amen.

WEEK 35: THE CHANGE AGENT! (GOD'S PRESENCE)

Luke 5:17, One day He was teaching; and there were some Pharisees and teachers of the law sitting there, who had come from every village of Galilee and Judea and from Jerusalem; and the power of the Lord was present for Him to perform healing.

A change is coming. There is so much healing that is needed in our land, government, emotions, and our bodies. We try to bring change through so many different ways but the good results are short-lived. What we need more of to bring change to our homes, churches, government, and the health of our bodies is God's presence. The scripture says, "The power of the Lord was present to Heal." Believe that we are going to see the change we need, as we submit and allow the power of God's presence (His Anointing) to be manifested where we are. People are hungry for this and it is time for the church and the people of God to put up the "out of order" or "do not disturb" signs over our lives, and allow the change to take place. Be healed, be delivered, get the wisdom you need, and be set free by God's presence! The change is coming, are you ready?

* * *

Builder's Prayer

Dear Lord, I am ready for Your change to come in the world and in my life. I praise You in advance for the freedom that Your presence gives. Thank you for healing, delivering, and changing my life in a way that brings glory to Your name. In Jesus name, I pray. Amen.

WEEK 36: YOU ARE AN OVERCOMER!

---

1 John 5:5, Who is the one who overcomes the world, but he who believes that Jesus is the Son of God?

Our church regularly fasts. During one of our fasts, we studied the book of James and 1 John. During a fast, you do not change GOD, He changes YOU! You must believe that you received the overcoming spirit, so you can carry out God's plan. You must believe that you are able to overcome: fears, old habits, sins, things that weigh you down, old hurts, challenges with your family, and not being able to trust people or God fully. You are an overcomer and the days of saying "this is just the way I am" or "it is what it is" will not work. You are an Overcomer!

* * *

Builder's Prayer
Dear Lord, Thank you for making me an overcomer! I am able to overcome all things with Your grace. In Jesus name, I pray. Amen.

WEEK 37: GET THE STUFF OUT!

Joshua 7:23, They took them from inside the tent and brought them to Joshua and to all the sons of Israel, and they poured them out before the Lord. Joshua could not move forward as a leader and as a person until he got the accursed thing out.

One of his guys, Achan, brought some items to the camp that were against God and defiled the camp. When they tried to go to the next level, they could not until they got the stuff out. As you move forward as a family and as an organization, there will be some things that God will require you to get out of your home, mouth, thoughts, and ministries. Allow God to send the Holy Spirit to examine your heart and then be bold enough to get the stuff out. Stuff like: unforgiveness, anger, rebellion, your tithe (if you are keeping it), the sin of omission (knowing to do right and not doing it), jealousy, idols, and relationships that are detrimental to what God is calling you to do. You are the only person who knows what stuff you need to put out of your home spiritually and tangibly. Get the stuff out!

* * *

Builder's Prayer

Dear Lord, Please help me to get the stuff out of my life that hinder my ability to go to the next dimension in You. Nothing is worth me missing Your direction for my life. Nothing is worth me missing the manifestation of Your Glory. In Jesus name, I pray. Amen.

WEEK 38: I AM SURE OF IT!

Philippians 1:6, For I am confident of this very thing, that He who began a good work in you will perfect it until the day of Christ Jesus.

Walk in assurance knowing that God is faithful to complete what He has started in you. If you have wavered, do not be discouraged. The Word of God has located you today! Remain faithful and go deeper into God's Word. Don't neglect fellowship with your fellow brothers and sisters. Isolation can be an enemy. You are a champion and you will finish! Get excited about your future!

* * *

Builder's Prayer
Dear Lord, I am excited about my future in You! Help me to stand firm and not lose heart as You continue to work on me in every area of my life. Your faithfulness is sure! In Jesus name, I pray. Amen.

WEEK 39: CHECK YOUR ASSOCIATIONS!

1 Corinthians 15:57, But thanks be to God, who gives us the victory through our Lord Jesus Christ. Are you having the kind of victory you know you should be having?

We all deal with life circumstances. When you are associated with the right person or people you will have the victory. Do not be deceived. Victory is more than waving a checkered flag. Victory is accomplished on the inside through Christ Jesus. This association tells me that no matter what I am facing God will accomplish what He desires in my life. You have the victory in and over your situation through Christ Jesus. If you are not feeling victorious today, check your associations. Remind yourself that you are victorious!

* * *

Builder's Prayer
Dear Lord, Help me to have Christ-focused associations. Thank you for making me victorious in You. Thank you for accomplishing Your Will in my

life and for keeping me from becoming distracted by things that are not of You. In Jesus name, I pray. Amen.

WEEK 40: PRAISE BREAKER!

Acts 16:25-26, But about midnight Paul and Silas were praying and singing hymns of praise to God, and the prisoners were listening to them; and suddenly there came a great earthquake, so that the foundations of the prison house were shaken; and immediately all the doors were opened and everyone's chains were unfastened.

When someone forgets the combination to their locker, they may need a bolt cutter to break into it. Once they open their locker, there is such freedom and relief in being able to get their belongings. In the scriptures, two men (Paul and Silas) were locked up in prison and bound with chains along with other inmates. They couldn't get out. These two men did not try to break out with bolt cutters. Instead, they focused their heart on Jesus and began to praise God for who He was in their lives. Regardless of their situation, God had been merciful to them. So they praised God relentlessly and their praise opened the doors and unfastened the chains around their feet. This is what praise will do! The Praise Breaker will open doors for you that were closed and loose the shackles of fear, depression, defeat, loneliness, sickness, poverty, and generational curses from around you. Begin to use your Praise Breaker to unlock the things God has for you. Free yourself and others around you from the obstacles in life!

* * *

Builder's Prayer

Dear Lord, I praise you anyway! In the midst of all that is going on around me and in my life, I still give You praise. You are the One Who makes a way out of no way. You are God over everything that threatens to keep me in bondage. In Jesus name, I pray. Amen.

WEEK 41: DO NOT LOSE HEART, YOU CAN MAKE IT!

---

2 Corinthians 4:16, Therefore we do not lose heart, but though our outer man is decaying, yet our inner man is being renewed day by day.

Y ou are healed! Your finances are increasing! You will carry out your divine purpose! Do not be discouraged today. You are more than a conqueror! If you are tired, get some rest, but do not lose heart!

* * *

Builder's Prayer
Dear Lord, I will not give up! You have already paid the price for me to be more than a conqueror. Thank you for Your strength and grace that keep me encouraged. In Jesus name, I pray. Amen.

WEEK 42: THE PACE HAS CHANGED!

Hebrews 12:1, Therefore, since we have so great a cloud of witnesses surrounding us, let us also lay aside every encumbrance and the sin which so easily entangles us, and let us run with endurance the race that is set before us.

We don't have much time. When a runner starts out with the crowd, everyone is running together. As the runner runs, he or she realizes that they cannot keep the same pace if they expect to accomplish their goal. They may run up some hills and through some valleys with this same pace. As a result, they may find themselves farther behind. You are running also. Sometimes life takes you up some hills and through some valleys but you keep running at the same pace. You must change your pace if you are going to fully accomplish God's will for your life. The speed of life has changed and the harvest is expanding! The Lord has called you to a place to run in ministry, in prayer, in your home, and in the marketplace. Consequently, the pace has changed. It's not that you are slow. It's just that the pace has changed.

Go ahead and write that book, record that song, start that business, answer the call on your life, increase your prayer time, or whatever God has placed in your heart to do! Go after the harvest with urgency! The pace has changed!

* * *

Builder's Prayer

Dear Lord, I need You to help me pick up the pace. Please give me the discernment that I need to recognize the changes in the season that require a greater pace from me. Thank you for enabling me to go after You with an urgency. In Jesus name, I pray. Amen.

WEEK 43: DON'T BE AFRAID TO CALL HEALING!

Acts 9:34, Peter said to him, "Aeneas, Jesus Christ heals you; get up and make your bed."

I mmediately he got up. We live in a world where people are sick in their bodies, relationships, finances, minds, and emotions. It has been this way for so long for whatever reason. If we are not careful, it will cause us to shrink in fear. Do not back down from the Word and the anointing that is on the inside of you. Begin to call healing to those sickly situations in your life. You may have to silence the noise around you and the noise from your past so that God can work through you. The more time you spend with God, people will see God's presence operating in and around you. Others will be attracted the kingdom. By faith, just call healing forth in Jesus Name. Do not walk in fear; spend time with the fearless one (Jesus) and watch your faith arise.

* * *

Builder's Prayer

Dear Lord, I am not afraid to call forth healing. I believe that You are a healer and that You want me healed and whole in my body and in my mind. Thank you God for healing me in every area of my life. In Jesus name, I pray. Amen.

WEEK 44: EXPOSE YOURSELF TO GREATNESS!

2 Kings 2:12, Elisha saw it and cried out, "My father, my father, the chariots of Israel and its horsemen!"

And he saw Elijah no more. Then he took hold of his own clothes and tore them in two pieces. This is an awesome story of a spiritual son being exposed to greatness. Elisha stood and watched his master, Elijah be taken up into heaven. He also observed Elijah divide the water and walk on dry ground just before that. Elisha was never the same after being exposed to greatness. The spirit of complacency or a "know it all" spirit did not rule in his life. As a result, Elisha's ministry and faith went to the next level. When you allow yourself to read new books, meet new people, visit new places, or learn from your spiritual leaders, God will expose you to new stuff and expand your territory. This will take faith, humility, and boldness. There are godly things and places you must allow yourself to be exposed to so that you can carry out your divine assignments. What was great last year is only average this year. It is time for a new and fresh revelation for your ministry, marriage, finances, business, etc. Do not be intimidated. Allow yourself to be exposed to greatness, because greatness is on the inside of you!

* * *

Builder's Prayer

Dear Lord, Please open new doors of opportunity for me to experience life on a greater level. Expand my thinking and vision to see You in a greater way in Your power. Help me to become greater in my walk with You. Thank you for breathing life into every area of my life. In Jesus name, I pray. Amen.

WEEK 45: THE CHANGE YOU NEED!

Matthew 28:1-2, Now after the Sabbath, as it began to dawn toward the first day of the week, Mary Magdalene and the other Mary came to look at the grave. And behold, a severe earthquake had occurred, for an angel of the Lord descended from heaven and came and rolled away the stone and sat upon it.

When we are on our life's journey, we can sometimes expect one thing but get something else. Most of us do not like change, especially when our minds and emotions are looking for something else. These two ladies in the scriptures prepared themselves to go and look at the body of Jesus in the tomb. While they were on their way, a change took place. There was an earthquake. Then an angel rolled the stone away and sat on the very thing that was holding the body inside. This is the change we all need! When we are set in our ways or our emotions have been affected by something, we can't see the truth and the opportunities in the struggle. God will cause an earthquake to happen in our lives through the Holy Spirit to move the blinders from our eyes. We need to see the situation differently so we can hear Him. The angel reminded them of what was really going on in this situation.

This is the change we all need. God, set off an earthquake in our spirits and roll the blinders away so we can hear again, see again, and live again!

* * *

Builder's Prayer

Dear Lord, Heal me in my mind and emotions where I hurt. Help me to see life differently where I'm not seeing life properly. Help me to hear you and your instructions for me. Thank you in advance for causing an earthquake in my spirit so I can see, hear, and live again! In Jesus name, I pray. Amen.

WEEK 46: TIME TO LEAVE!

Hebrews 11:27, By faith he left Egypt, not fearing the wrath of the king; for he endured, as seeing Him who is unseen.

Fearing the unknown can cause a person to stay where they are, even if it's a bad place. If we are not careful, fear of the unknown can be a little king over our lives. Moses was willing to endure whatever came because he had seen and heard from the invisible God. Moses knew it was time to leave. It is time for you to stop letting your fears, hurts, doubts, and negative thoughts (little kings) prevent you from leaving the old and embracing the new. It won't be easy. You must keep your eye on the King of Kings. He will get you through it. It is time to leave.

* * *

Builder's Prayer
Dear Lord, I believe that You will give me the wisdom to know when it is time to leave a situation. I trust You to close the necessary doors in order to direct me to the purpose You have for my life. Help me to go boldly in that direction. In Jesus name, I pray. Amen

WEEK 47: I AM HERE NOW!

Luke 24:15, While they were talking and discussing, Jesus Himself approached and began traveling with them.

There are times when we feel that God is not near. Life can hit so hard at times that it brings confusion to your soul man. In the scriptures, two men who had just seen their leader, Jesus, die a brutal death on the cross were walking and discussing the situation with each other. They could not believe it and they felt abandoned. While they were walking in this confused state, Jesus drew near. Wow, the things Jesus is attracted to! This is so comforting to know that our God is near us, especially during those times that are confusing. God is with you! He has brought you peace, regardless of that confused situation. Even the confused situation where Jesus died on the cross brought healing to the world. God is near and you have peace!

* * *

Builder's Prayer
Dear Lord, Thank you for the peace that You so graciously give to me in times of chaos when my life does not make sense. Thank You for comforting my soul. In Jesus name, I pray. Amen.

WEEK 48: BE STRENGTHENED!

Isaiah 40:29, He gives strength to the weary, and to him who lacks might He increases power.

If you are feeling weak in your mind, body, or emotions, you are in a great position for strength today. Weakness is God's opportunity to be strong in you. Life has pulled your old strength, but God will renew your strength today. This is a seed of strength to you as God moves mightily where you need Him!

* * *

Builder's Prayer

Dear Lord, I am thankful that Your strength prevails during my moments of weakness. I will not give up. In Jesus name, I pray. Amen.

WEEK 49: RUN...RUN...RUN!

Hebrews 12:1, Therefore, since we have so great a cloud of witnesses surrounding us, let us also lay aside every encumbrance and the sin which so easily entangles us, and let us run with endurance the race that is set before us.

God designed you for purpose and He has placed everything you need on the inside of you to live it out. Like any race, there will be things that you will have to deal with, just because of life itself. But the things you must watch out for are those parasites.

Parasites are those spirits that attach themselves to you with added weight through bad habits, unfruitful conversations, and even hurts. The thing about a parasite is, it needs a host or place to get its energy from and will thrive on the energy you give it. You have heard of the saying, "Anything you give energy to grows"...which will also slow you down or restrict your progress. Those things that restrict your progress can grow through our conversations or our own lust. You must make the decision to lay those things aside or stop doing those things (habits or sins) that will impede your progress. You don't have much time before the checkered flag is waved. You must finish the race God designed for you!

* * *

Builder's Prayer
Dear Lord, Help me to lay aside anything in my life that is hindering me from fulfilling my purpose in You. Help me to stay focused on finishing the race You designed for me. I want to finish strong! In Jesus name, I pray. Amen.

WEEK 50: I MUST STEP DOWN!

John 3:30, He must increase, but I must decrease.

John the Baptist was out doing what he believed God had called him to do. God was truly involved in what he was doing. John the Baptist was truly not operating in his own strength. He was a man who was submitted unto God. If a man is already operating at this level, why would he have to say, "He must increase, but I must decrease". This is a great example for us today. Many of us are doing what God wants us to do, but we have to remind ourselves to step aside so our flesh won't rule. We need Jesus to continue to increase in our relationships, marriages, careers, courtrooms, the overseeing of our children, ministry, and every area of our lives. John recognized his limitations in advancing God's agenda and knew he needed to step aside (decrease). If you are going to truly carry out God's plan and agenda in your life, you must step down.

* * *

Builder's Prayer
Dear Lord, Help me to decrease so that You may increase. Let all that I do bring glory to Your name. In Jesus name, I pray. Amen.

WEEK 51: TAKE OVER WITH YOUR BELIEF!

Mark 9:23, And Jesus said to him, "'If You can?' All things are possible to him who believes."

The God of all grace is standing to answer our prayers if we would only believe. I know situations and circumstances come to make us doubt, and to see that situation as impossible because change has not come. The Lord Jesus Christ has been given the power over heaven and earth so we can execute His will. We must begin to take over those impossible areas in our lives by just believing God. The enemy want us to stop believing God. I want to encourage you to take over that situation through your belief. Jesus said, "All things are possible to him who believes." Wow...we have to believe this and begin to believe! When we start believing, we begin to take over the demonic influence around the situation. Begin to do it today! Lord, I believe you today for (**state whatever you need from God**) and begin to speak about what you are believing for.

* * *

Builder's Prayer

Dear Lord, Help me to believe. Strengthen my belief so that I can take down demonic strongholds over the areas in my life that need to be free. Thank You for Your freedom-giving power in my life. In Jesus name, we pray. Amen.

WEEK 52: THE STRUGGLE IS OVER!

Jeremiah 1:6-7, Then I said, "Alas, Lord God! Behold, I do not know how to speak, because I am a youth." But the Lord said to me, "Do not say, 'I am a youth,' because everywhere I send you, you shall go, and all that I command you, you shall speak."

We all struggle with doing and walking into what God has called us to do. We struggle because of fear of rejection, fear of failure, or lack of confidence. Be encouraged! Friend, the struggle is over! Do not accept your excuses another day. God has truly equipped you with His ability to carry out His tasks in the earth. God once called a man named Jeremiah to do something for Him. Jeremiah immediately looked inward at his inability instead of looking upward at God's ability. God would not allow Jeremiah to make excuses because the call was bigger than him. God wanted Jeremiah to trust in His ability instead of his own.

You must know that the only way you are going to fail is by not trying at all. You must walk in faith and trust His Word. Let's go for it! The struggle is over! Don't battle another day with whether you should or shouldn't. The answer is yes!

Yes, your marriage can be better! Yes, you should start that business! Yes, you should forgive your brother! Yes, you should get involved in a church! Yes, you should apply for that promotion! Yes, you should clean up your credit! Yes, you should take care of your body! I declare the blessing of the Lord over you this year and for your heart to be more sensitive to the things of God and the direction He wants you to go.

* * *

Builder's Prayer

Dear Lord, Please help me to let go of my fears and insecurities so that I can follow Your plans for my life! Help me to rise above my past failures so I can embrace Your best for my life. Thank you that the struggle is over! In Jesus name, I pray. Amen.

Dear Lord, Thank you for building me so that I can build others. In the name of Jesus Christ, I pray. Amen.

94268470R10055

Made in the USA
Columbia, SC
22 April 2018